THE BOOK OF

FINGER
FOODS

THE BOOK OF
FINGER FOODS

HILAIRE WALDEN

Photographed by
PATRICK McLEAVEY

HPBooks

ANOTHER BESTSELLING VOLUME FROM HPBOOKS

HPBooks
Published by The Berkley Publishing Group
A division of Penguin Putnam Inc.
375 Hudson Street
New York, New York 10014

Home Economist: Alison Austin

First edition: December 1999

The Penguin Putnam Inc. World Wide Web site address is
http://www.penguinputnam.com

Library of Congress Cataloging-in-Publication Data

Walden, Hilaire.
        The book of finger foods / Hilaire Walden; photographed by
Patrick McLeavey.–
1st ed.
p.   cm.
ISBN 1-55788-325-4(tp)
1.   Appetizers   I. Title: Finger foods. II. Title.
TX740.W217 1999
641.8'12–dc21   99-047402
                                     CIP

Printed and bound in Spain

10   9   8   7   6   5   4   3   2   1

CONTENTS

FOREWORD

The Book of Finger Food contains an imaginative selection of eclectic dishes for food that can be eaten easily in the fingers, in just one or two bites. The recipes are not intimidating or complicated, with extra emphasis being placed on flavor and overall eating enjoyment. No special skills are required, with many of the dishes being ready to eat in a short time. The recipes are based on cuisines from around the world, sometimes in new guises.

The majority of the recipes in *The Book of Finger Food* are ideal for today's casual entertaining, but there are also recipes for more formal, elegant affairs. And there are dishes to suit all tastes.

The introduction offers invaluable advice and helpful tips for planning parties, choosing dishes, creative presentation, sleek serving, and organization of drinks, all of which contribute to successful, relaxed occasions for both guests and hosts. However, the recipes in *The Book of Finger Food* are not just for parties. They also make tasty first courses, picnic fare and packed meal choices. A selection of the recipes can provide a light meal, accompanied by a salad, or form part of a buffet.

INTRODUCTION

A party should be enjoyable and relaxed for the host as well as the guests. The only way that this can happen, unless the event is an impromptu affair, is by forward thinking and planning and by making lists and a detailed time plan. Begin by deciding on the date, the type of occasion, the budget, and the number of guests. Then settle down to the vital practical and organizational aspects.

CHOICE OF FOOD
Time spent on the careful selection of the food to be served will pay dividends later both in terms of the enjoyment of the food and the calmness and confidence of the host. It will allow the host to spend time with the guests rather than being confined to the kitchen.

Consider the colors, textures and flavors of the food that you

intend to offer and try to provide contrasts, such as in texture – some crisp, some soft, some smooth and some coarse. Avoid having too many similar flavors, such as a menu of all spicy dishes like Mexican, Indian and Thai. Combine light and more substantial items, and include a mixture of ingredients – meat, fish, vegetables, cheese and egg, plus some plain items, as well as one or two varieties that can be placed around the room for people to 'nibble' at, such as Savoury Palmiers. Try not to repeat the ingredients, by serving two chicken dishes for example. For the guests' convenience, and to keep the floor clean, it should be possible to eat all the items in one or two bites.

Do not be too ambitious; it is far better to keep the food simple than to attempt dishes that are overly complicated or that you do not feel at ease preparing. If you want to serve recipes that you have not tried before, make them at least once in advance. Allow enough time to do all

the shopping so that there is not too much to buy close to the event.

Think about how you will cook, store and heat the food. Serve a balance of hot and cold dishes and plan to have some dishes that need to be broiled, some fried and others that can be cooked in the stove. It is a good idea to start with a cold recipe that can be placed out on plates before the guests arrive.

Choose a high proportion of items that can be fully or at least partly prepared, preferably frozen, in advance and keep to the minimum recipes that require last-minute attention.

PLANNING
When working out cooking times, remember that stoves are less efficient when laden, and that large pans will take longer to heat up than normal family-sized pans. Assess your equipment and utensils. Make sure that you have enough pots and pans and that they are large enough for the quantities that you will be making; borrow some if necessary, but do make sure that they will fit into the stove.

Refrigerator space will be at a premium with prepared items, ingredients, wines and soft drinks all requiring to be kept cool. Ask friends to lend a shelf or two in their refrigerators, or buy some cool boxes and ice blocks.

Bear in mind what help, if any, there will be in the kitchen both in advance and during the occasion; call on friends or family to ease the load. Also, remember to arrange for help

taking the food and drink around, choosing people who can be relied upon to keep circulating and not to linger over conversations.

Provide plenty of serving plates that are large enough that they do not have to be returned to the kitchen frequently for replenishing, but not so large that the food begins to look messy. When choosing large plates, consider their weight when loaded with food, bearing in mind that someone will have to carry them.

Have a good supply of aluminum foil or large paper napkins for covering serving trays. Position cocktail sticks around the room (with dishes to hold used sticks), and plenty of good quality cocktail-size paper napkins. In the kitchen, you need to stock up with garbage bags, kitchen paper, and dishtowels.

Think about how and where the dishes for serving hot food will be warmed. If the stove is full, plates and dishes can be put to warm over a saucepan of water, bowl, or sink of hot water (don't forget to wipe the bottom of the plate or dish before using). An electric heated trolley or hot tray will, obviously, do the job well.

Schedule time into the preparations for arranging the room, clearing and cleaning up the kitchen and, most importantly, ample time for getting yourself ready and relaxing before the guests arrive.

QUANTITIES

A variety of factors affect the quantities that will be needed, such as the time of day, the time of year, the type of occasion, who is coming, how many guests there will be (the more there are the less they will eat proportionately), and their appetites. For a finger food party, offer at least six varieties, and allow eight to ten items per person. For pre-supper eats, allow about five items per person.

PREPARATION

Empty the garbage, clear as much work surface as possible and keep surfaces clean and free of clutter while working. Assemble all the ingredients and equipment that will be needed before starting and work on the conveyor-belt principle. For example, when preparing Shrimp Toasts, prepare as much of the shrimp mixture that will be needed, lay out all the slices of bread, spread with the topping, sprinkle over the sesame seeds then cut all the slices into triangles.

PRESENTATION

Appearances do matter, even if the food is given only a glance before being eaten. Plain plates show off food better and look cleaner than decorative, patterned ones. Food will be cramped on small plates, so opt for those that are larger, but not king-size. For extra impact, look for varied shapes; secondhand shops or car boot sales can unearth interesting finds. Unusual surfaces and containers look effective – mirrors, shiny black plates, aluminum foil-covered trays or other flat surfaces, and cookie tin lids, pieces of metal with any rough edges carefully covered with sticky tape, wooden trays, a bread board or cheese board, wicker baskets, or even a hollowed-out loaf can all be eye-catching.

For convenience and speed when adding garnishes, keep them simple, relevant and edible, and prepare them well in advance. A complicated garnish can soon lose its appeal when the plates are handed round and the food is removed. A sprinkling of finely chopped fresh herbs or some small herb sprigs can be added easily at the last minute.

SERVING

Keep cold food tightly covered until the last minute so that it looks fresh. Offer only a couple of varieties at a time, and ensure a steady flow of dishes out of the kitchen in tune with the rate at which it they are being eaten.

DRINKS

Offer a choice of wine but keep the choice limited. Often just one red wine and one white wine will be sufficient, plus some beer. Try to be a little more imaginative than offering just orange juice as a non-alcoholic alternative; make a non-alcoholic punch instead.

One bottle of wine should provide 5-6 glasses, a liter bottle gives 6-8 glasses but, obviously the size of the glasses are a factor.

To chill wine, line tubs with plastic sacks and fill with a mixture of ice and water. Keep in a cool place. A 28lb (12.6kg) bag of ice should chill a case of wine in about 1 hour, longer on hot days. Move chilled bottles to the top as you put more in, or transfer them to cool boxes or bags and pack around with newspaper that has been chilled in the freezer. Wine can be opened ahead and the corks pressed back in.

STUFFED FRESH DATES

20 fresh dates
½ cup (4oz/115g) cream cheese
¼ cup (1oz/25g) pistachio nuts, finely chopped
1 tablespoon chopped stem ginger
1 tablespoon chopped fresh mint
salt and freshly ground black pepper
small mint leaves, to garnish

With point of a small, sharp knife, cut a slit along length of each date. Ease out the pits.

In a bowl, mix together remaining ingredients, except garnish. Fill dates with a little cheese mixture. Chill for 1 hour. Garnish with mint leaves and serve.

Makes 20

STUFFED CELERY

4 large sticks celery, cut diagonally into 5 pieces
celery leaves, to garnish
FILLING
½ cup (2oz/50g) pine nuts
2oz (50g) cilantro leaves
1 plump clove garlic, crushed
½ cup (2oz/50g) freshly grated Parmesan cheese
2 tablespoons olive oil
freshly ground black pepper

To make filling, preheat broiler. Spread pine nuts on a baking sheet and toast lightly, stirring frequently. Leave to cool then chop finely. With a pestle and mortar, crush toasted nuts, cilantro, and garlic together to a nubbly texture. Work in Parmesan then oil. Season to taste with pepper.

Divide filling among celery pieces. Garnish with celery leaves and serve.

Makes 20

— CAMEMBERT BAKED IN A BOX —

1 whole ripe but reasonably firm
  Camembert, in a box
1 clove garlic, halved
a little fruity white wine
grissini and/or crudités, to serve

Preheat oven to 400F (200C). Remove cheese from box and discard the wrapping. Return cheese to box. Rub cut sides of garlic over top of cheese. With a sharp knife, slice top off Camembert then replace it on top of cheese.

Pierce 6 holes in top of cheese with a skewer and trickle in a few drops of wine. Replace lid of box. Bake cheese for 25-30 minutes, or until hot and bubbling. Remove box lid and top slice of cheese. Place box of cheese on a plate and surround with grissini and/or crudités. Serve immediately while cheese is melted and runny.

Serves 6-8

ASIAN CRACKERS

½ red capsicum, deseeded and chopped
½ yellow capsicum, deseeded and chopped
2 teaspoons grated fresh root ginger
2 tablespoons toasted sesame seeds
2 tablespoons sesame oil
2 tablespoons light soy sauce
few drops of chili sauce
40 prawn crackers

In a bowl, mix chopped capsicums, ginger, sesame seeds, sesame oil, and soy sauce together. Season with chili sauce to taste. Cover and keep cool for up to 4 hours.

Transfer capsicum mixture to a cool serving bowl. Stand bowl on a serving plate and surround with prawn crackers.

Makes 40

SAVORY PALMIERS

about 12oz (350g) puff pastry, thawed if frozen
4-6 tablespoons anchoiade (anchovy paste)
2 tablespoons chopped fresh basil
freshly ground black pepper
vegetable oil for greasing

On a lightly floured surface, roll out dough to an 8x10in (20x25cm) rectangle. Chill for at least 30 minutes. Mix two-thirds of anchoiade with basil and pepper. Spread anchoiade mixture over pastry. Fold the two long sides over pastry to meet in center. Press flat.

Spread remaining anchoiade on top. Fold in half and press down firmly. Slice thinly. Grease baking sheets, and place slices cut-side up on baking sheets. Chill for 30 minutes. Preheat oven to 425F (220C). Bake palmiers for 10 minutes. Turn them over and bake for a further 4-5 minutes until golden. Cool slightly on a wire rack and serve warm.

Makes about 24

TUNA CROSTINI

24 slices from thin French loaf
oil from jar of sun-dried tomatoes in oil, or
 virgin olive oil for brushing
7oz (200g) can tuna in brine, drained
2 tablespoons lemon mayonnaise
4 sun-dried tomatoes in oil, drained and finely
 chopped
2 tablespoons chopped fresh basil
2 tablespoons chopped fresh flat-leaf parsley
squeeze of lemon juice, to taste
salt and freshly ground black pepper
TO GARNISH
coarsely chopped capers
sliced black olives

Preheat oven to 350F (180C). Brush both sides of bread with oil. Place slices on a baking sheet and bake for about 10 minutes until pale golden brown. Cool on a wire rack.

In a bowl, mix together tuna, mayonnaise, sun-dried tomatoes, basil, and parsley. Add lemon juice, and salt and pepper to taste. Spread tuna mixture over crostini. Garnish some of the crostini with capers and some with black olives.

Makes 24

— CHEESE CORNMEAL SQUARES —

1 cup (4oz/115g) all-purpose flour
1 cup (4oz/115g) cornmeal
1 tablespoon baking powder
1 tablespoon chopped fresh chives
salt and freshly ground black pepper
⅓ cup (3oz/85g) butter, melted
1 egg, beaten
⅔ cup (5fl oz/150ml) sour cream
½ cup (2oz/50g) grated Swiss cheese

Preheat oven to 425F (220C). Grease an 8in (20cm) square cake pan. In a bowl, stir together flour, cornmeal, baking powder, chives, and salt and pepper. Make a well in center. Pour in butter, egg, and sour cream. Stir together to make a smooth, wet dough.

Spread dough evenly in pan. Cover with cheese. Bake for 20-25 minutes until set, and golden on top. Leave to cool in pan then invert on to a chopping board. Cut into approximately 1½in (4cm) squares. Serve warm or cold, cheese-side up.

Makes about 25

FRUITY SAUSAGE BALLS

1lb (450g) good quality, well-flavoured sausages
1½ cups (9oz/250g) pitted prunes
scant 1 cup (3½oz/100g) hazelnuts, chopped
1¼ cups (10fl oz/300ml) chicken stock
3½oz (100g) redcurrant jelly
lemon juice, to taste
salt and freshly ground black pepper

Preheat oven to 350F (180C). Slit sausage skins and remove meat. Chop half prunes and mix with sausage meat and hazelnuts. Form into 20 small balls. Place on a baking sheet. Bake for 40 minutes.

In a blender, purée remaining prunes, the stock, and redcurrant jelly. Add lemon juice, and salt and pepper to taste. Pour into a small saucepan and bring just to a boil. Transfer to a warm serving dish. Put sausage-meat balls on a warm serving plate and stand dish of sauce in center.

Makes 20

— CHEESE & TOMATO KABOBS —

8oz (225g) pecorino cheese, cut into about
  ½in (1cm) cubes
24 small cherry tomatoes
3 tablespoons extra virgin olive oil
1½ tablespoons lemon juice
1 tablespoon chopped fresh parsley
1 tablespoon chopped fresh oregano
freshly ground black pepper

Thread cheese and cherry tomatoes
alternately on to toothpicks. Put in a
shallow, non-metallic dish.

Whisk together olive oil, lemon juice, fresh
herbs, and plenty of coarsely ground black
pepper. Pour over kabobs, and turn them to
coat in dressing; cover and marinate in the
fridge for 2 hours.

Makes 24

— HOME-DRIED PEARS & CHEESE —

2 large, ripe Comice or Bosc pears, peeled, halved,
 cored and thickly sliced
12oz (350g) Stilton or other blue cheese (not Danish
 or Roquefort), rind removed, cut into bite-size
 cubes

Preheat oven to 225F (110C). Spread pears
on a jelly roll pan. Put in oven for 4-6 hours
until flesh feels firmer when pressed and,
when cut, edges curl and are browned
slightly. Cool completely.

Cut pear slices into bite-size pieces. Spear a
piece of pear and a piece of cheese with
toothpicks.

Makes about 36

STILTON WITH WALNUT COOKIES

8oz (225g) Stilton without rind or other blue cheese, crumbled
small bunch of fresh flat-leaf parsley, finely chopped
4 sticks celery, finely chopped
freshly ground black pepper
flat-leaf parsley leaves (optional), to garnish
COOKIES
¼ cup (1oz/25g) walnut halves
½ cup (4oz/115g) unsalted butter, chopped
2 cups (8oz/225g) all-purpose flour

Using a fork, mash cheese with parsley, celery, and black pepper. Cover and chill. To make cookies, preheat broiler. Spread walnuts on a baking sheet and toast lightly, stirring nuts frequently. Leave to cool, then chop nuts. Rub butter into flour and black pepper until mixture resembles fine bread crumbs. Stir in nuts. Form into a dough with 3-4 tablespoons water. Knead lightly on a lightly floured surface. Cover and chill for 30 minutes.

Preheat oven to 350F (180C). Grease baking sheets. On a lightly floured surface, roll out dough until thin. Use a 1½in (4cm) cutter to cut into rounds. Re-roll trimmings as necessary. Transfer to baking sheets and bake for 10-15 minutes, or until browned. Remove to a wire rack to cool. Serve cookies topped with Stilton mixture, and garnished with parsley, if you like.

Makes about 80

PARMESAN CRISPS

melted butter for greasing
8oz (225g) **Parmesan cheese**, finely grated
2 tablespoons very finely chopped fresh chives

Preheat oven to 400F (200C). Cover baking sheets with non-stick baking parchment. Sprinkle cheese in mounds on baking sheets and flatten slightly with a fork to 2in (5cm) rounds.

Bake for 2½ minutes. Sprinkle Parmesan rounds with chives and bake for a further 30 seconds. Remove Parmesan rounds from oven. Leave for 2 minutes to become crisp. Using a metal palette knife, transfer to a wire rack to cool.

Makes about 16

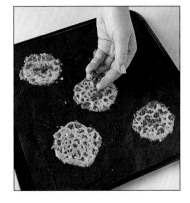

CREAMY CHEESE PUFFS

2 tablespoons (1oz/25g) butter
2 cloves garlic, crushed and finely chopped
½ cup (4oz/115g) mascarpone cheese
2 teaspoons prepared English mustard
salt and freshly ground black pepper
6 tablespoons freshly grated Parmesan cheese
12oz (350g) puff pastry, thawed, if frozen
1 egg, beaten

Melt butter in a small saucepan, add garlic and cook over a medium heat until softened and golden. Leave until cooled but not set. Place mascarpone cheese in a large bowl, add the mustard, salt and pepper, and 4 tablespoons of Parmesan cheese. Strain in melted butter and beat together. On a lightly floured surface, roll out pastry to 14x9in (35x22.5cm).

Cut pastry into 4 strips lengthwise; cut each strip into 6. Put a heaped teaspoonful of cheese mixture in center of 12 pieces. Brush pastry edges with beaten egg. Put a piece of pastry on top and press edges together firmly to seal. Transfer to a baking sheet. Brush top of puffs with egg and sprinkle with remaining Parmesan. Chill for 30 minutes. Preheat oven to 425F (220C). Bake for 10-15 minutes, or until puffed and golden. Serve immediately.

Makes 12

CRISP RICOTTA GNOCCHI

2lb (900g) ricotta cheese
1¼ cups (5oz/150g) all-purpose flour
1 cup (3oz/85g) freshly grated Parmesan cheese
1 extra large egg
salt and freshly ground black pepper
1⅔ cups (8 oz/225g) coarse semolina

In a bowl, mash ricotta, flour, Parmesan, egg, and salt and pepper together with a fork until evenly blended. Cover and chill for at least 2 hours. Shape cheese mixture into about 30 walnut-size balls and roll in semolina to coat evenly.

Preheat oven to 350F (180C). Bring a large saucepan of salted water to simmering point. Carefully add balls in batches. As soon as balls rise to surface, remove with a slotted spoon and put in a greased shallow baking dish. Bake for about 20 minutes, or until a thin crust forms. Serve hot or at room temperature.

Makes 30

· GOATS' CHEESE & LEEK PARCELS ·

2 tablespoons (1oz/25g) unsalted butter
8oz (225g) trimmed leeks, finely chopped
4oz (115g) goats' cheese, crumbled
2oz (50g) sun-dried tomatoes in oil, drained and
   finely chopped
freshly ground black pepper
8 sheets phyllo pastry, each about 12x18in
   (30x45cm)
melted butter for brushing
sesame seeds for sprinkling

Preheat oven to 400F (200C). Heat butter in a large non-stick skillet. Add leeks and fry over a medium heat until softened. Transfer to a bowl to cool. Stir in goats' cheese, tomatoes, and pepper. Place a pastry sheet on counter. Brush lightly with melted butter. Put another sheet next to it, overlapping the long edges by about 1in (2.5cm) to make 24x18in (60x45cm) rectangle. Butter lightly. Repeat with 2 more phyllo sheets.

Put 1 teaspoon cheese mixture at 2in (5cm) intervals on pastry. Cover with remaining pastry, buttering as before. Press between mounds of filling with side of hand. Use a large, sharp knife to cut into small parcels. Seal edges by pressing firmly. Brush with butter, sprinkle with sesame seeds, and bake for 8-10 minutes.

Makes about 48

FETA FINGERS

6oz (175g) feta cheese, crumbled
3oz (85g) chopped fresh flat-leaf parsley
2oz (50g) chopped fresh dill
freshly ground black pepper
1 package phyllo pastry
about 9oz (250g) melted butter for brushing
sesame seeds and/or poppy seeds for sprinkling
   (optional)

Preheat oven to 400F (200C). Oil a baking
sheet. In a bowl, mix feta cheese, parsley,
dill, and pepper. Working with 1 sheet of
phyllo at a time (keep remaining sheets
covered), cut into 5x8in (12.5x20cm) strips.
Place 1 strip on counter with short end
towards you. Brush with melted butter.
Cover with a second strip.

Put a teaspoon of cheese mixture at bottom
of strip. Fold in ¼in (0.5cm) along each
side. Roll up. Transfer to baking sheet,
brush with melted butter and sprinkle with
sesame and/or poppy seeds, if using. Repeat
with remaining cheese mixture and pastry.
Bake for 10 minutes, or until crisp and
golden. Serve warm.

Makes about 30

PROVENÇAL PUFFS

12oz (350g) puff pastry, thawed if frozen
2-3 tablespoons tapenade
12oz (350g) cherry tomatoes, sliced
4oz (115g) firm goats' cheese or feta cheese, chopped
freshly ground black pepper
thyme leaves, to garnish

On a lightly floured surface, roll out pastry to 14x9in (35x22.5cm). Using a large, sharp knife, cut into 4 lengthwise and 8 crosswise strips. Put pastry rectangles, a little apart, on 2 dampened baking sheets. Cover and chill for at least 30 minutes.

Preheat oven to 425F (220C). Dot a little tapenade in center of each pastry rectangle. Put tomato slices on top then add chopped cheese. Add plenty of black pepper. Bake for 1-5 minutes or until risen and golden. Sprinkle with thyme leaves. Transfer to a wire rack. Serve warm or cold.

Makes 32

– CHEESE & WATERCRESS PUFFS –

1 bunch watercress, about 3oz (85g)
1 cup (8fl oz/225ml) milk
2 eggs, beaten
2 tablespoons (1oz/25g) butter, melted, plus extra for
   greasing
1 cup (4oz/115g) all-purpose flour
2-3 teaspoons chopped fresh parsley
salt and freshly ground black pepper
4oz (115g) fairly firm goats' cheese, cubed

Preheat oven to 425F (220C). Butter about
36 mini muffin pans. Put in oven to heat.
Reserve a few small watercress sprigs for
garnish. Mix remainder of watercress with
milk, eggs, butter, flour, parsley, and salt and
pepper in a blender until smooth.

Pour batter into muffin cups. Divide cheese
between cups. Bake for 15-20 minutes until
risen and golden.

Makes about 36

— ONION & CHEESE TARTLETS —

2½ cups (10oz/300g) all-purpose flour
½ cup (2oz/50g) cornmeal
⅓ cup (1½ oz/40g) freshly grated Parmesan cheese
freshly ground black pepper
generous ¾ cup (7oz/200g) butter
3 egg yolks
1lb (450g) Spanish onions, halved and thinly sliced
1¼ cups (10fl oz/300ml) crème fraîche
4oz (115g) feta cheese, crumbled
4 whole sun-dried tomatoes, halved and thinly sliced
8 oil-cured pitted black olives, halved and
   thinly sliced
about 60 basil leaves, to garnish

In a bowl, stir flour, cornmeal, Parmesan, and black pepper together. Rub in ¾ cup (6oz/175g) of the butter until mixture resembles crumbs. Stir in egg yolks and enough water to make a dough. Cover and chill for at least 30 minutes.

Meanwhile, in a large skillet heat remaining butter, add onions and fry, stirring occasionally, until beginning to caramelize. Pour in crème fraîche. Bring to a boil and bubble for 15-20 minutes, or until reduced, stirring occasionally. Cool.

On a lightly floured surface, roll out pastry until thin. Using a 2in (5cm) plain cutter, cut into rounds. Use to line mini tartlet pans. Prick bases and chill for 20 minutes. Preheat oven to 400F (200C). Bake pastry cases for 15-20 minutes. Remove to a wire rack to cool.

Stir feta and black pepper into onion mixture. Transfer tartlet cases to baking sheets.

Fill each tartlet case with 1 teaspoon onion mixture. Add a piece of sun-dried tomato and olive. Return to oven for 10 minutes. Garnish each tartlet with a basil leaf.

Makes about 60

ARTICHOKE FRITTATA

6 artichokes preserved in oil, thinly sliced
3 cloves garlic, unpeeled
3 tablespoons oil from artichokes, or olive oil
9 extra large eggs
3 tablespoons crème fraîche or heavy cream
salt and freshly ground black pepper
3 tablespoons chopped fresh flat-leaf parsley
about ½ cup (2oz/50g) grated Gruyère cheese, for
  sprinkling (optional)

Preheat broiler. Spread artichoke slices and garlic on a baking sheet and cook under broiler until evenly lightly charred. Remove skin from garlic, crush cloves, and chop finely. In a 12in (30cm) non-stick skillet, heat oil. In a bowl, beat eggs with crème fraîche or cream, and salt and pepper. Add artichokes, garlic, and parsley.

Pour egg mixture into pan and cook very slowly for about 15 minutes until body of eggs is just set and top is liquid. Sprinkle cheese over, if using. Put pan under broiler for 1-2 minutes, or until top is set or cheese has melted. Let cool, if you like. Run a palette knife around edge of frittata to loosen it and slide frittata from pan. Cut frittata into small diamond shapes.

Makes about 60

ARNOLD BENNETT SLICES

3 eggs, separated
1 tablespoon freshly grated Parmesan cheese
1 tablespoon heavy cream
freshly ground black pepper
4oz (115g) Finnan haddock
1 teaspoon lemon juice
2 tablespoons heavy cream, beaten
1 tomato, skinned, deseeded and chopped
chili pepper

Preheat oven to 375F (190C). Line a 8x12in (20x30cm) jelly roll pan with baking parchment. Stir egg yolks, Parmesan, heavy cream, and pepper together. Beat egg whites until stiff and carefully fold into yolk mixture. Turn mixture into pan and bake for 10-12 minutes. Allow to cool. In a small saucepan, put fish and just enough water to cover. Simmer for 10 minutes then drain well and discard skin.

Chop fish finely and mix with lemon juice. Fold into heavy cream, with tomato and black and chili pepper to taste. Invert omelette on to baking parchment. Carefully remove lining paper. Cut omelette in half. Spread each half with haddock mixture, almost to edges. With help of paper, roll up like a jelly roll. Slice each into 10 rolls.

Makes 20

SCOTCH EGGS

5oz (150g) fresh bread crumbs
4 tablespoons finely chopped fresh tarragon
6 tablespoons capers, coarsely chopped
10oz (300g) pitted green olives, chopped
1¼lb (550g) mild goats' cheese
salt and freshly ground black pepper
6oz (175g) ciabatta bread, made into crumbs
¾ cup (3oz/85g) chopped walnuts
8 eggs, hard cooked
sunflower oil for deep-frying
2 tablespoons mayonnaise
2 teaspoons Worcestershire sauce
2 teaspoons sun-dried tomato paste
squeeze of lemon juice
cilantro sprigs, to garnish

In a bowl, mix bread crumbs, tarragon, capers, olives, goats' cheese, and black pepper until thoroughly combined. In a separate bowl, stir ciabatta crumbs and walnuts together. Divide cheese mixture into 8 pieces. Mould each piece smoothly around an egg. Roll in walnut mixture. Chill, uncovered, for 30 minutes.

Heat oil in a deep-fat fryer to 375F (190C). Deep-fry eggs in batches for about 2 minutes, or until golden. Drain on paper towels. Cool. Slice eggs in half. Scoop yolks into a bowl. Add mayonnaise, Worcestershire sauce, sun-dried tomato paste, lemon juice, and salt and pepper to taste. Spoon into a pastry bag fitted with a large star tube. Pipe filling into cavities in eggs. Garnish with cilantro sprigs.

Makes 16

— STUFFED CHERRY TOMATOES —

30 cherry tomatoes
2 tablespoons (1oz/25g) unsalted butter
4 eggs, lightly beaten
2 tablespoons heavy cream
1 tablespoon finely chopped fresh dill
1 tablespoon finely chopped green olives
3 tablespoons freshly grated pecorino or
  Parmesan cheese
salt and freshly ground black pepper
sprigs of dill, to garnish

Slice off tops of tomatoes. Using a melon baller or small teaspoon, carefully scoop out insides of tomatoes; take care not to pierce skin. (Use tops and tomato flesh in sauces or soups.) Stand tomatoes upside down on paper towels. Melt butter in a non-stick saucepan. Add eggs and stir over a low heat for 1 minutes. Add cream and cook, stirring, until only very lightly cooked. Remove from heat and stir in dill, olives, and one-third of cheese. Season with salt and pepper.

Preheat broiler to high. Using a teaspoon, spoon egg mixture into tomatoes, forcing mixture in with back of the spoon. Put on a baking sheet. Sprinkle remaining cheese over tomatoes. Grill for 30 seconds. Garnish with dill sprigs. Serve warm or cold.

Makes 30

CHINESE TEA EGGS

24 quails' eggs
2 tablespoons jasmine tea leaves
2 teaspoons light soy sauce
1½in (4cm) cinnamon stick
1½ star anise
salt
ground Szechuan pepper and sea salt, to serve

Put eggs into a large saucepan. Cover with plenty of water and bring slowly to a boil. Cook for 45-60 seconds. Transfer to a colander and cool under running cold water.

Simmer tea leaves in 2½ cups (20fl oz/550ml) of water in a small, covered pan. Strain out leaves. Tap eggs gently with back of a spoon to crack in a crazed pattern. Put in a pan in a single layer. Add tea and remaining ingredients, except Szechuan pepper and sea salt. If necessary, add more water to cover eggs. Slowly bring to a boil, cover and simmer gently for 20 minutes.

Remove pan from heat and leave eggs in water for 6 hours or overnight. Just before serving, pour away the liquid and carefully peel eggs. Mix Szechuan pepper with an equal amount of sea salt in a small serving bowl and serve with eggs.

Makes 24

- ASPARAGUS EGGS ON BRIOCHE -

16 slim green asparagus spears
8 slices brioche
3 tablespoons (1½oz/40g) butter, melted
1 tablespoon finely chopped fresh chives
salt and freshly ground black pepper
4 extra large eggs, beaten
4 tablespoons crème fraîche

Preheat oven to 425F (220C). Cut 2in (5cm) long tips from asparagus and discard woody stalks. Bring a saucepan of water to a boil. Add asparagus tips and quickly return to a boil. Boil for 30 seconds. Drain, refresh under running cold water and drain again. Pat dry and set aside. Using a 2in (5cm) cutter, stamp out 2 circles from each brioche slice. Brush with 2 tablespoons butter. Bake for 3-4 minutes or until golden.

Heat remaining butter in a non-stick saucepan. Beat the chives, and salt and pepper into eggs and pour into the pan. Stir over a low heat for 3-4 minutes until just set. Remove from heat and stir in crème fraîche. Divide among brioche toasts and garnish with asparagus tips.

Makes 16

THAI SPRING ROLLS

2oz (50g) cellophane vermicelli, soaked in warm
　　water for 20 minutes
8 crisp lettuce leaves, finely shredded
1lb (450g) cooked large shrimp, peeled and halved
　　across
1oz (25g) fresh mint, chopped
2oz (50g) fresh cilantro, chopped
about 1 tablespoon Thai fish sauce, to taste
1 tablespoon grated fresh root ginger
4 tablespoons lime juice
1 tablespoon sesame oil
freshly ground black pepper
8x6in (20x15cm) rice flour wrappers
cilantro sprigs, to garnish

Drain vermicelli and use scissors to cut into
short lengths. Put into a bowl and mix with
remaining ingredients, except wrappers and
garnish. Dip 1 wrapper at a time in hot
water for 30 seconds, or until just softened.
Put a heaped tablespoon shrimp mixture on
a wrapper slightly nearer to you than center.

Fold sides of wrapper over filling then roll
wrapper up tightly around filling. Repeat
with remaining filling and wrappers. Cover
and refrigerate until required. Arrange on a
large serving plate and garnish with cilantro
sprigs.

Makes 20

DEEP-FRIED FISH BITES

3 tablespoons chopped mixed fresh herbs such as
  fennel, dill, parsley, mint
1 cup (4oz/115g) dried bread crumbs
1¼lb (550g) skinned flounder fillets, cut into
  2½x½in (6x1cm) strips
⅓ cup (1½oz/40g) all-purpose flour
2 eggs, beaten
vegetable oil for deep-frying
SAUCE
3 tablespoons Greek-style yogurt
6 tablespoons mayonnaise
2-3 tablespoons lime juice
2 tablespoons chopped fresh cilantro or parsley
1 tablespoon each chopped capers and gherkins
salt and freshly ground black pepper

To make sauce, stir yogurt, mayonnaise, and
lime juice together. Add herbs, capers,
gherkins, and salt and pepper. Cover and
chill.

Toss together herbs, bread crumbs, and salt
and pepper. In batches, put the fish in a
large bag, add flour, and toss to coat fish in
flour. Dip fish in egg then roll in herbed
bread crumbs. Heat oil in a deep fryer to
375F (190C). Deep-fry fish in batches for
about 2 minutes, or until golden. Drain on
paper towels. Serve warm with sauce.

Makes about 60

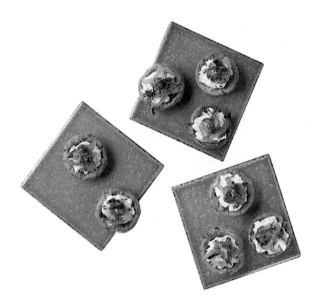

— GRAVADLAX CROUSTADES —

6 slices medium-thick light rye bread, crusts removed
½ cup (4oz/115g) unsalted butter, melted
about 5 tablespoons mascarpone cheese or
　sour cream
8oz (225g) gravadlax, finely chopped
fresh dill, to garnish

Preheat oven to 350F (180C). Roll out each slice of bread as thinly as possible. Using a 2in (5cm) cutter, stamp out rounds. Brush rounds on both sides with melted butter then press into mini tartlet tins. Bake for 15-20 minutes, or until crisp and brown. Remove to a wire rack and cool.

Spoon mascarpone cheese or sour cream into each croustade case. Top with gravadlax then a little of the sauce that comes with gravadlax. Garnish with fresh dill.

Makes 24

—— SPINACH & SHRIMP ROLLS ——

1 cup (8oz/225g) Thai fragrant rice
1in (2.5cm) piece fresh root ginger, grated
2 teaspoons Thai fish sauce
4 scallions, finely chopped
8oz (225g) large spinach leaves, stalks removed
8oz (225g) peeled, cooked, large shrimp, chopped
salt

Put rice in a saucepan with scant 2 cups
(15fl oz/425ml) water. Bring to a boil, cover
and cook for 10 minutes. Remove from heat
and leave to cool for 5 minutes, without
lifting lid. Remove lid. Stir in the ginger,
fish sauce, and scallions. Leave until cold.
Add spinach to a large saucepan of boiling
water for a few seconds. Drain, rinse in cold
water and drain again. Spread leaves out in
a single layer on a cloth to dry.

Spread 4 sheets plastic wrap on counter. Lay
spinach on top to make 4 rectangles about
6x10in (15x25cm), overlapping as
necessary. Mix shrimp and salt into rice and
spread over leaves. Press down with wetted
hands. Starting from long edge, roll up
leaves tightly, enclosing filling. Wrap
tightly in plastic wrap. Chill for at least
1 hour. Remove wrap and cut each roll into
10 slices to serve.

Makes 40

SMOKED SALMON ROLLS

1 cup (8oz/225g) full-fat cream cheese
2½-3 tablespoons finely chopped fresh chives
about 1 tablespoon lemon juice
salt and freshly ground black pepper
about 9oz (250g) sliced smoked salmon
lemon wedges (optional), to serve

Beat cheese, then beat in chives, lemon juice, a little salt, and plenty of pepper. Cover and chill for at about 4 hours.

Spread cheese mixture over slices of smoked salmon and roll up tightly. Chill. Using a large, sharp knife, cut rolls into ¼in (0.5cm) slices. Arrange, cut-side up, on a cold serving platter. Add lemon wedges, if you like, and serve.

Makes about 70

—— SMOKED SALMON SUSHI ——

2 sheets toasted nori seaweed
1 teaspoon wasabi powder or horseradish cream
½oz (15g) pickled ginger
6oz (175g) sliced smoked salmon
¼ cucumber, cut into matchsticks
Japanese soy sauce for dipping
SUSHI RICE
¾ cup (6oz/175g) Japanese rice
3 tablespoons rice vinegar
1in (2.5cm) piece kelp (optional)
pinch of sugar
salt

To prepare sushi rice, put rice, vinegar, kelp,
if using, and 1 cup plus 2 tablespoons
(9fl oz/250ml) water in a saucepan. Cover
and simmer until water has evaporated.
Leave, still covered, for 10 minutes. Discard
kelp, if used, and season with sugar and salt.

Lay a nori sheet on baking parchment.
Spread a thin layer of rice to 3 edges but
leaving 2in (5cm) clear at far edge. Sprinkle
with wasabi, or spread with horseradish.
Arrange line of ginger across near edge,
then top with salmon slice and a few sticks
of cucumber. Using baking parchment, roll
up sushi to a tight cylinder. Leave to set for
1 hour. With a very sharp knife, cut into
½in (1cm) slices. Serve with a small bowl of
soy sauce.

Makes about 20

—— MARYLAND CRAB CAKES ——

5oz (150g) cooked white crabmeat
3oz (85g) cooked skinless white fish such as cod or
   haddock, finely flaked
3½oz (100g) tortilla chips, finely crushed
2 tablespoons chopped fresh cilantro
1 tablespoon ginger juice (see Note)
1 tablespoon lime juice
scant ½ cup (3½oz/100g) mayonnaise
1 tablespoon Dijon mustard
freshly ground black pepper
2 eggs, beaten
vegetable oil for frying

Mix crab, white fish, half the tortilla chips, the cilantro, ginger and lime juices, mayonnaise, mustard, and black pepper together. Cover and chill for at least 1 hour. With floured hands, form into 24 balls, then flatten them into patties. Dip in beaten egg then coat in remaining tortilla chips.

Fry patties in hot oil in batches in a non-stick skillet for 2 minutes each side, until crisp and golden. If you like, leave to cool. Reheat, uncovered, for 10 minutes at 400F (200C).

Makes 24

NOTE: To make ginger juice, grate 1½oz (40g) fresh root ginger then squeeze to give 1 tablespoon.

— GINGER BISCUITS WITH CRAB —

2 cups (8oz/225g) all-purpose flour
salt and freshly ground black pepper
1½ teaspoons baking powder
½in (1cm) fresh root ginger, grated
1 cup (8fl oz/225ml) heavy cream
6-7 tablespoons milk
melted butter for brushing and greasing
6oz (175g) fresh white crabmeat
2 teaspoons lemon juice
⅔ cup (5fl oz/150ml) sour cream

Preheat oven to 400F (200C). Grease a baking sheet. In a bowl, stir together flour, salt and pepper, baking powder, and ginger. Lightly work in cream and enough milk to make a soft dough. Turn on to a lightly floured surface and knead gently once or twice. With finger-tips, press carefully to ½in (1cm) thick. Using a 1in (2.5cm) plain cutter, stamp out biscuits. Transfer to baking sheet. Brush tops with melted butter. Bake for 10 minutes, or until risen and golden. Transfer to a wire rack to cool.

Meanwhile, in a bowl, stir together crabmeat, lemon juice, and salt and pepper. Split biscuits in half. Add a little sour cream to bottom halves. Top with crab mixture, replace tops and serve.

Makes about 14

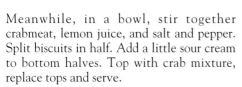

GOLDEN CRAB TARTS

1 quantity pastry (see page 30)
1 egg, beaten
3 tablespoons chopped fresh flat-leaf parsley
pinch of saffron threads, crushed
⅔ cup (5fl oz/150ml) heavy cream
squeeze of lemon juice
salt and freshly ground black pepper
8oz (225g) white crabmeat, flaked
fresh flat-leaf parsley, to garnish

On a lightly floured surface, roll out pastry thinly. Stamp out about 60 rounds using a 2in (5cm) cutter. Use to line mini tartlet pans. Prick bases well and chill for at least 30 minutes. Preheat oven to 400F (200C). Bake pastry cases for 10 minutes, or until golden. Cool on a wire rack, if you like.

Meanwhile, beat egg, parsley, and saffron into cream. Season with lemon juice, and salt and pepper. Divide crabmeat among pastry cases. Spoon in some saffron cream. Return to oven for 5-10 minutes. Serve warm, garnished with parsley.

Makes about 60

——— SHRIMP TOASTS ———

9oz (250g) peeled fresh shrimp
3 scallions, chopped
6 basil or cilantro leaves
1 teaspoon grated fresh root ginger
small piece of orange rind
2 teaspoons cornstarch
½ teaspoon sesame oil
2 teaspoons rice wine or dry sherry
1 egg white
salt and freshly ground black pepper
6 slices from good quality large loaf, crusts removed
about 2 tablespoons sesame seeds
groundnut oil for frying
lime wedges, to serve

Put all ingredients except bread, sesame seeds, and groundnut oil in a blender or food processor. Mix to a fairly smooth paste. Spread paste on bread and sprinkle with sesame seeds. Cut into triangles or fingers, or into crescents using a cookie cutter.

Heat ½in (1cm) depth groundnut oil in a large skillet until a cube of bread browns in 40 seconds. Add bread in batches, paste side down. Fry for 1 minute then turn over and fry for 15-20 seconds until golden. Drain on paper towels. Keep warm and uncovered. Serve with lime wedges.

Makes about 24

— CURRIED SHRIMP ON NAAN —

1 tablespoon groundnut oil
4 scallions, finely chopped
1 clove garlic, crushed
2 teaspoons fragrant curry powder
12oz (350g) cooked, peeled shrimp, coarsely chopped
4 teaspoons plain yogurt
4 teaspoons mango chutney
salt and freshly ground black pepper
2 large naan breads, each about 5oz (150g)
cilantro, to garnish

Heat oil in a skillet, add scallions, and garlic and fry for 2 minutes. Stir in curry powder and shrimp. Cook gently for 2 minutes. Remove pan from heat and stir in yogurt, chutney, and salt and pepper.

Heat bread according to package instructions. Cut bread into small squares. Top with a little shrimp mixture and garnish with cilantro leaves.

Makes 60

— MUSSELS ON GARLIC BREAD —

20 slices from small baguette, 1in (2.5cm) thick
1 large clove garlic, halved lengthways
3 tablespoons (1½oz/40g) butter
3 shallots, finely chopped
⅔ cup (5fl oz/150ml) medium-bodied dry white wine
14oz (400g) small mussels, cleaned
2 tablespoons chopped fresh basil
large pinch of saffron threads
1¼ cups (10fl oz/300ml) heavy cream
salt (if necessary) and freshly ground black pepper
fresh basil, to garnish

Preheat oven to 375F (190C). Remove some of the crumb from center of baguette slices. Rub remaining bread with the cut side of 1 piece of garlic. In a large saucepan, heat butter, then add shallots and remaining garlic. Fry for 5 minutes, until soft. Pour in wine and bring to a boil.

Add mussels, cover, and steam for 3-4 minutes, until mussels have opened. Discard any that remain closed. Remove mussels from shells. Strain liquid and return to rinsed pan. Add basil, saffron, and cream. Boil until reduced to a coating consistency. Season to taste. Return mussels to pan and warm for 1-2 minutes over a medium heat. Bake bread 5-8 minutes, until lightly colored and just crisp. Spoon mussels and sauce on to bread slices. Garnish with basil.

Makes 20

— MEDITERRANEAN MUSSELS —

2 shallots, very finely chopped
1 clove garlic, finely crushed
4 tablespoons red pesto
freshly ground black pepper
½ cup (4oz/115g) butter, softened
⅓ cup (3fl oz/85ml) dry white wine
sprig of rosemary
6lb (2.75kg) mussels, cleaned
¼ cup (1oz/25g) freshly grated Parmesan cheese
1oz (25g) ciabatta bread, made into crumbs
finely chopped fresh parsley, to garnish

Beat shallots, garlic, red pesto, and black pepper into butter. Set aside. Add wine and rosemary to a large saucepan and bring to a boil. Add mussels, cover, and simmer for 3-5 minutes, or until mussels open; shake the pan occasionally. Discard any mussels that remain closed.

Preheat broiler. Line a large broiler pan with crumpled foil. Remove the top shells from mussels and stand bottom shells in foil. Divide flavored butter among mussels. Stir together Parmesan and ciabatta crumbs. Sprinkle over mussels. Broil for about 5 minutes, or until golden. Sprinkle finely chopped parsley over and serve.

Makes about 30

—— SEARED SCALLOP KABOBS ——

48 bay or small scallops
16 rosemary sprigs, or small bamboo skewers
rocket leaves, to serve
DRESSING
4 tablespoons walnut oil
2 tablespoons sherry vinegar
2oz (50g) sun-dried tomatoes in oil, chopped
leaves from 1 small bunch of basil, chopped
freshly ground black pepper

To make dressing, whisk together walnut oil and vinegar. Stir in sun-dried tomatoes and basil. Season with black pepper. Set aside.

If using bamboo skewers, soak in water for 30 minutes. Thread 3 scallops on each rosemary sprig or bamboo skewer. Place in a shallow dish, pour dressing over and turn scallops to coat in dressing. Leave in a cool place for 30 minutes. Preheat broiler. Remove scallops from marinade and cook under hot broiler for about 2 minutes, turning occasionally, and basting with remaining marinade. Serve on a bed of rocket leaves.

Makes 16

PINK SEAFOOD CROÛTES

¼ cup (2oz/50g) butter, melted
8 thin slices bread
FILLING
1 tablespoon butter
1 clove garlic, crushed
2 scallions, chopped
1 tablespoon chopped fresh tarragon
5oz (150g) fresh mixed seafood cocktail
4 tablespoons lemon mayonnaise
1 tablespoon sun-dried tomato paste
freshly ground black pepper

Preheat oven to 400F (200C). Butter 16 small tartlet pans with some melted butter. With a 2in (5cm) cutter, stamp rounds from bread slices. Fit into tartlet pans, pressing in well. Brush with remaining butter. Bake for 10-15 minutes, or until crisp and golden. Transfer to a wire rack to cool.

To make filling, in a small pan, heat butter, add garlic, and fry until softened. In a bowl, mix scallions, tarragon, seafood, mayonnaise, sun-dried tomato paste, garlic, and black pepper. Divide among the tartlet cases.

. *Makes 16*

CHICKEN BREAST ROLLS

4 boneless chicken breasts, skinned
⅓ cup (3oz/85g) ricotta cheese
4 tablespoons black olive tapenade
4 sun-dried tomatoes in oil, chopped
freshly ground black pepper
8 spinach leaves
⅔ cup (5fl oz/150ml) chicken stock
⅔ cup (5fl oz/150ml) medium-bodied dry white wine

Put each chicken breast between 2 sheets of plastic wrap. Using a rolling pin, beat thinly. Remove wrap. Beat together ricotta, tapenade, sun-dried tomatoes, and plenty of pepper. Spread over chicken.

Cover each piece of chicken with 2 spinach leaves. Roll up each breast into a thin roll. Secure with wooden toothpicks. Wrap in foil and chill for 30 minutes.

Pour stock and wine into a deep skillet that chicken rolls will just fit. Heat to a simmer, add foil-wrapped chicken, cover and poach for 5 minutes. Remove from heat and let chicken cool in liquid for 30 minutes. Remove and cool completely. Discard foil and cut rolls into ½in (1cm) slices. Arrange on a serving plate.

Makes 20-25

— CHICKEN & HAM WONTONS —

1lb (450g) skinless chicken fillets, chopped
4oz (115g) Parma ham, chopped
1½in (4cm) piece fresh root ginger, grated
small handful of fresh cilantro
1 clove garlic, crushed
2 scallions, chopped
1 egg white
freshly ground black pepper
24 rectangular wonton wrappers
groundnut oil for deep-frying

Put chicken, ham, ginger, cilantro, garlic, scallions, egg white, and black pepper in a food processor. Mix to a coarse purée so that ingredients hold together but there are discernible pieces.

Put a heaped teaspoonful of chicken mixture in center of one wrapper. Brush edges of wrapper with water. Fold corners to center and pinch together. Pinch along seams to seal. Put on a floured baking sheet. Repeat with remaining wrappers. Chill for up to 6 hours, wrapped in plastic wrap if you like. Preheat a deep pan of oil to 350F (180C). Deep-fry wontons in batches for 3-4 minutes until puffed and golden. Drain on paper towels and keep warm.

Makes 24

— STICKY CHICKEN LOLLIPOPS —

15 chicken wings, about 1½lb (700g) total weight
1 teaspoon coriander seeds
¾ teaspoon cardamom seeds
5 tablespoons tomato catchup
2 tablespoons maple syrup
1 tablespoon allspice
2 teaspoons paprika
pinch dried red chili flakes
grated rind of 1 small lime

Cut off chicken wing tips at joint; discard.
Using a sharp knife, cut through skin and
tendons on either side of bone. Hold bone
end and scrape meat down to other end.

In a dry, small, heavy skillet heat coriander
and cardamom seeds until fragrant. Crush in
a pestle and mortar and mix with remaining
ingredients.

Place chicken pieces in a large non-stick
roasting pan. Pour catchup mixture over
chicken and turn and stir until evenly
coated. Leave to marinate in a cool place for
1 hour. Preheat the oven to 425F (220C).
Bake chicken for 45 minutes, until charred
and sticky, turning pieces occasionally.
Serve immediately.

Makes 15

MINI CHICKEN TIKKA

1¼ cups (10fl oz/300ml) plain yogurt
2 cloves garlic, crushed
2 teaspoons grated fresh root ginger
2 teaspoons tomato paste
grated rind and juice 1 lime
2 teaspoons garam masala
¼ teaspoon each of ground cumin, coriander, and
  ground chilies
salt and freshly ground black pepper
1lb (450g) chicken breast meat, cut into
  bite-size pieces
RAITA
½ cucumber, finely chopped
1¼ cups (10fl oz/300ml) Greek-style yogurt
2 tablespoons finely chopped fresh mint

In a bowl, stir together yogurt, garlic, ginger, tomato paste, lime rind and juice, spices, and salt and pepper. Stir in chicken, cover and refrigerate overnight.

To make raita, dry cucumber and mix with yogurt, mint, and salt and pepper. Chill until required. Just before serving, preheat broiler. Remove chicken from marinade and spread in a roasting pan. Cook for 6-8 minutes, or until reddish-brown and cooked through. Spear with toothpicks and serve with raita.

Makes 24

FRAGRANT CHICKEN

14oz (400g) chicken breast meat, cut into thin strips
2 cloves garlic, crushed
1 fresh red chili, deseeded and chopped
2 pinches of saffron threads
4 tablespoons olive oil
salt
handful of mint leaves
juice of 1 large lemon

Thread chicken strips on to wooden skewers. Place in a shallow non-metallic dish. Put garlic, chili, saffron, olive oil, salt, and most of the mint and lemon juice in a blender. Mix to a purée. Pour over chicken, turn to coat in purée and leave to marinate for 30 minutes.

Preheat a ridged grill pan and oil lightly. Add skewers with marinade clinging to chicken strips. Cook on pan for 3-4 minutes each side, or until golden and cooked through. Mix remaining mint and lemon juice and sprinkle over chicken just before serving.

Makes about 20

— CRISP DUCK PANCAKE ROLLS —

2 duck breasts, each about 8oz (225g)
2 cloves garlic, crushed
1in (2.5cm) piece fresh root ginger, grated
2 tablespoons clear honey
2 tablespoons dry sherry
about ⅔ cup (5fl oz/150ml) Chinese plum sauce
2 cups (8oz/225g) all-purpose flour
salt and freshly ground black pepper
2 eggs, beaten
2½ cups (20fl oz/550ml) milk and water mixed
sesame oil for frying
1 cucumber, peeled, halved, deseeded and cut in
   2in (5cm) lengths
1 bunch scallions, cut in 2in (5cm) long strips
3 tablespoons chopped fresh cilantro

Slash duck breasts 3 times each with a sharp knife. In a shallow dish, mix garlic, ginger, honey, and sherry, and marinate duck in a cool place for 1 hour. Preheat oven to 400F (200C).

Place duck on a rack over a roasting pan and roast for 15 minutes. Let cool. Remove fat and skin from duck, and spoon off fat from juices in roasting pan. Stir juices left in pan into plum sauce.

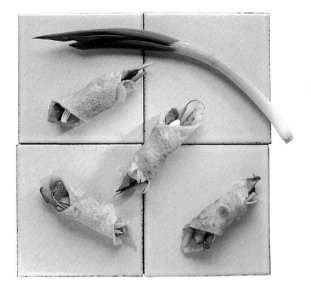

Sift flour, and salt and pepper into a bowl. Make a well in center, add eggs and milk mixture and gradually draw in flour to make a smooth batter. Leave for 30 minutes. Heat and lightly oil a 6in (15cm) skillet. Pour in a small ladleful of batter, tip and rotate pan so batter flows evenly over base. Cook for 1 minute, or until brown. Turn over and cook for 30 seconds. Remove and repeat with remaining batter to make about 12 pancakes. Leave to cool.

Slice duck then cut into thin strips. Mix with the cucumber, scallions, and cilantro.

Cut pancakes into quarters. Spread plum sauce over each quarter. Top with a small spoonful of duck mixture. Fold pancakes tightly into rolls and secure with toothpicks.

Makes 48-60

— TURKEY & CRANBERRY ROLLS —

2 tablespoons (1oz/25g) butter
1 shallot, finely chopped
3oz (85g) fresh bread crumbs
1 tablespoon chopped fresh flat-leaf parsley
1 tablespoon fresh thyme
1 teaspoon finely grated lemon rind
1 egg, beaten
salt and freshly ground black pepper
4x4oz (115g) turkey breast fillets
2oz (50g) cranberries, thawed if frozen
8oz (225g) thinly-sliced rindless bacon

Preheat oven to 400F (200C). Heat butter in a skillet and fry shallot until soft. In a bowl, stir together bread crumbs, shallot, parsley, thyme, lemon rind, egg, and salt and pepper. Place each turkey fillet between sheets of plastic wrap and beat with a rolling pin to flatten. Season with pepper. Spread stuffing over each turkey fillet. Arrange cranberries down length of stuffing.

Roll up each fillet from a long edge. Wrap in bacon, overlapping slices slightly. Roast for 20-25 minutes, or until bacon is crisp and turkey cooked through. Cut into 1in (2.5cm) slices. Spear with toothpicks. Serve warm or cold.

Makes 32

– PARMA-WRAPPED ASPARAGUS –

8 sheets of phyllo pastry
¼ cup (2oz/50g) unsalted butter, melted
½ cup (2oz/50g) freshly grated pecorino or
  Parmesan cheese
freshly ground black pepper
8 thin slices Parma ham
8 fat asparagus spears, trimmed
sesame seeds for sprinkling
lemon wedges, to serve

Preheat oven to 450F (230C). Lay one phyllo sheet on counter; keep remaining sheets covered. Brush phyllo sheet with melted butter and fold in half.

Sprinkle cheese and black pepper over pastry and place a slice of ham on top. Place asparagus across ham. Roll up pastry enclosing ham and asparagus.

Brush rolls with butter and sprinkle sesame seeds over. Transfer to a non-stick baking sheet. Repeat with remaining ingredients. Bake for 10 minutes until crisp and golden. Serve hot or at room temperature, with lemon wedges.

Makes about 60

MERGUEZ 'CRACKERS'

8oz (225g) fresh spinach
¼ cup (2oz/50g) butter, melted
3oz (85g) merguez or chorizo sausage cut into
    ¼in (5mm) cubes
⅓ cup (3oz/85g) ricotta cheese
salt and freshly ground black pepper
about 5oz (150g) phyllo pastry, cut into 3in
    (7.5cm) squares

Cook spinach in a covered pan until leaves
wilt. Drain well and squeeze out as much
water as possible. Coarsely chop and leave
to cool.

Preheat oven to 400F (200C). Butter a
baking sheet with a little butter. Fry
merguez or chorizo without any fat until
lightly browned. Drain on paper towels and
set aside to cool. In a bowl, mix together
spinach, merguez or chorizo, and ricotta
cheese. Season to taste with salt and pepper.

Stack phyllo squares in pairs, buttering each
square. Put a little spinach mixture in center
of each stack, roll up and pinch pasty ends
to resemble Christmas crackers. Place on
the baking sheet. Bake for 10-12 minutes
until crisp and golden. Serve warm.

Makes about 24

—— MINI 'TOAD-IN-THE-HOLE' ——

2 cups (8oz/225g) all-purpose flour
2 cups (16fl oz/450ml) milk
2 eggs, beaten
4 tablespoons wholegrain mustard
salt and freshly ground black pepper
4 tablespoons vegetable oil
20 good quality herbed chipolatas or other thin
  sausages

Put flour, milk, eggs, mustard, and salt and
pepper in a food processor or blender and
mix until evenly combined. Leave in a cool
place for at least 30 minutes.

Preheat oven to 425F (220C). Lightly brush
mini muffin pans with oil. Cut sausages into
pieces that will fit in muffin cups. Put a
piece of sausage in each muffin cup and
cook in the oven for 15 minutes, or until
beginning to brown.

Working with 1 pan at a time, quickly pour
about 1 tablespoon batter over each sausage
piece and return to the oven for
15-20 minutes, or until risen and golden.
Serve warm.

Makes about 60

MOROCCAN MEATBALLS

4 tablespoons sunflower oil
1 small onion, finely chopped
1 clove garlic, finely crushed
1¾ cups (14oz/400g) ground lamb
2oz (50g) fresh bread crumbs
1 teaspoon each ground cumin, coriander, and
   paprika
2 tablespoons each chopped fresh parsley and
   cilantro, finely chopped
2 tablespoons capers, finely chopped
1 tablespoon lemon rind
salt and freshly ground black pepper
flour for coating
paprika for sprinkling
yogurt and cilantro dip (see page 74), to serve

Heat 1 tablespoon of the oil in a skillet. Fry onion and garlic until soft. Cool. Pass meat through grinder several times. Knead in bread crumbs, onion, garlic, spices, herbs, capers, lemon rind, and salt and pepper. Cover and set aside for at least 2 hours.

Preheat broiler. With floured hands, form meat mixture into about 24 small balls. Heat remaining oil in a large skillet and fry meat balls in batches, shaking pan, for 5 minutes or until evenly browned. Drain on paper towels. Sprinkle with paprika and serve with dip.

Makes about 24

PORK NUGGETS

1¾lb (800g) boneless lean pork, cut into 1in
  (2.5cm) cubes
1oz (25g) cilantro leaves
3 cloves garlic, peeled
1¼in (3cm) piece fresh root ginger, sliced
1 lemon grass stalk, outer layers removed
grated rind of 1 lime
large bunch of scallions
2 large fresh red chilies, deseeded
2 tablespoons soy sauce
2 tablespoons clear honey
2 tablespoons white wine vinegar
2 tablespoons Thai fish sauce
2 tablespoons sesame oil
14fl oz (400ml) can coconut milk
lime wedges, to serve

Put pork in a shallow non-metallic dish.
Place half the coriander, the garlic, ginger,
1¼in (3cm) lemon grass, lime rind, and
remaining ingredients except coconut milk
in a blender and process finely. Scrape over
pork and stir pork to coat thoroughly. Cover
and refrigerate overnight. Remove pork
from marinade; thread 2 cubes of pork on
each wooden toothpick. Reserve marinade.

Preheat broiler. Broil pork nuggets for 4-5
minutes a side, brushing occasionally with
some of the marinade. Meanwhile, scrape
remaining marinade into a skillet, add
coconut milk and remaining lemon grass.
Boil briskly until thick. Discard lemon grass.
Chop remaining cilantro and add to sauce
with any remaining marinade. Serve hot
with pork, accompanied by lime wedges.

Makes about 30

PORK & MANGO SATAY

1lb (450g) lean pork, cut into bite-size cubes
2 tablespoons soy sauce
2 teaspoons sesame oil
1 teaspoon each ground cumin, coriander, cardamom
   and grated fresh root ginger
2 ripe mangoes, peeled and pitted
SATAY SAUCE
1 small onion, very finely chopped
2 cloves garlic, crushed
2½ teaspoons grated fresh root ginger
1 teaspoon very finely chopped lemon grass
2oz (50g) creamed coconut, chopped
4 tablespoons crunchy peanut butter

Put pork in a bowl. Mix together soy sauce, sesame oil, and spices. Stir into pork. Cover and marinate for at least 4 hours, stirring occasionally. To make sauce, in a saucepan, slowly bring all the ingredients plus 1¼ cups (10fl oz/300ml) water to a boil, stirring until coconut dissolves. Add more water if necessary. Keep sauce warm.

Preheat broiler. Cut mangoes into same size pieces as pork. Remove pork from marinade and thread a cube each of pork and mango on to small skewers. Broil for about 10 minutes, turning halfway through. Serve pork and mango skewers with hot sauce in a bowl.

Makes about 25

CHINESE BEEF

2in (5cm) piece fresh root ginger, grated
6 star anise
7-8 tablespoons dark soy sauce
⅔ cup (5fl oz/150ml) rice wine or dry sherry
8oz (225g) fillet steak
3 shallots, finely chopped
1 clove garlic, finely crushed
3 tablespoons sesame oil
8oz (225g) red plums, pitted and chopped
5 tablespoons sweet sherry
lime juice and Tabasco sauce, to taste
12oz (350g) small new potatoes, in ¾in (2cm) slices
fresh cilantro, to garnish

Mix together half the ginger, the star anise,
4 tablespoons soy sauce, and rice wine or
sherry. Pour over beef, cover and marinate
for 8 hours, turning beef occasionally. Cook
shallots and garlic in 1 tablespoon sesame
oil until soft but not colored. Add plums,
remaining ginger, sweet sherry, and
3 tablespoons soy sauce. Boil rapidly until
syrupy. Add lime juice, Tabasco sauce, and
additional soy sauce to taste. Purée in a
blender, or sieve. Warm through before
serving. (Any remaining sauce can be kept
covered in a fridge for several days.)

Preheat oven to 425F (220C). Roast beef on
top shelf for 25 minutes for rare, 35 minutes
for medium. Meanwhile, toss potatoes in
remaining sesame oil. Bake on middle shelf
for about 45 minutes, or until tender,
turning once during cooking. Cool then
thinly slice beef. Arrange some beef on each
warm potato base. Add a little warm plum
sauce, and garnish with cilantro.

Makes 60

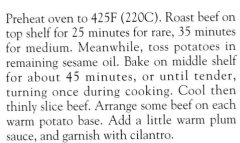

- WALNUT BREAD, HAM & SALSA -

1 loaf walnut bread, cut into ½in (1cm) slices
2 tablespoons olive oil
6oz (175g) ham, cut off the bone into 15 slices
½ cup (2oz/50g) walnuts, lightly toasted and finely chopped
fresh parsley or basil, to garnish
SALSA VERDE
3 tablespoons each chopped fresh mint, cilantro, and basil
1 clove garlic, chopped
2 tablespoons Dijon mustard
3 anchovy fillets
1 tablespoon capers
¼ cup (2fl oz/50ml) olive oil
juice of ½ lemon

To make salsa verde, put all the ingredients into a blender and mix until smooth. Cover and chill. Preheat broiler. Brush bread slices with oil. Put under broiler for about 1 minute or until lightly toasted.

Place a slice of ham on each piece of toast. Top with a spoonful of salsa verde then sprinkle chopped walnuts over. Cut into smaller pieces, if you like. Garnish with parsley or basil.

Makes 15-30

BEET ROULADE

10oz (300g) cooked beets
2 teaspoons grated onion
¾ teaspoon ground cumin
2 tablespoons (1oz/25g) butter, melted
3 eggs, separated
salt and freshly ground black pepper
FILLING
⅔ cup (5fl oz/150ml) crème fraîche or heavy cream,
  lightly whipped
3 tablespoons horseradish relish
about 2 teaspoons lemon juice
about 1 teaspoon sugar

Preheat oven to 375F (190C). Line and grease a 9x13in (23x33cm) jelly roll pan. Put beets, onion, cumin, butter, egg yolks, and salt and pepper in a blender and mix to a purée. Whisk egg whites until stiff peaks form. Stir 2 tablespoons into beet mixture, then carefully fold in remainder. Spread in prepared pan and bake for 15 minutes or until just set in center.

Invert on to a sheet of baking paper on a wire rack. Carefully remove lining paper in strips. Cover with a clean dish towel until cold. To make filling, combine all the ingredients, adding lemon juice and sugar to taste. Cut roulade in half widthwise. Spread filling over each half. Starting with a long side, roll up each piece tightly. Trim edges. Using a large, sharp knife, cut into about ¾in (2cm) slices.

Makes about 30

TOMATO CALZONE

3¼-3½lb (1.5kg) well-flavored tomatoes, peeled,
  deseeded and chopped
salt and freshly ground black pepper
2 cloves garlic, crushed
1 tablespoon olive oil
1 quantity risen pizza dough (see page 86)
3oz (85g) fontina, halloumi or goats' cheese, cut
  into 36 cubes
small handful basil leaves, torn
beaten egg, to glaze

Put tomatoes in a colander, sprinkle salt
over and leave to drain.

In a large saucepan, cook garlic in oil for 2-3
minutes. Add tomatoes and cook until
thick, stirring frequently. Season with salt
and pepper. Set aside until cold. Preheat
oven to 425F (220C). Punch down dough.
Break into 6 pieces. Halve these pieces then
cut each piece into 3 to make 36 pieces. On
a lightly floured surface, roll out each piece
of dough to an oval ⅛-¼in (3-5mm) thick.
Put a heaped teaspoon of tomato mixture on
half of each oval. Add a cube of cheese and
scatter some basil over.

Fold uncovered half of dough oval over the
filling to meet opposite edge. Press edges
together then mark with floured fork tines.
Cut 2 slashes in top of each calzone and
brush with beaten egg to glaze. Bake for 15-
20 minutes until brown and crisp around
edges.

Makes 36

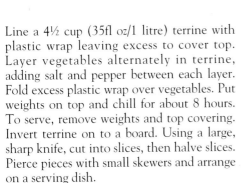

RATATOUILLE TERRINE

1 plump clove garlic, finely crushed
4 tablespoons oil from jar of sun-dried tomatoes, or
  virgin olive oil
2 teaspoons pesto
6 large plum tomatoes, cored and halved lengthways
salt and freshly ground black pepper
3 large yellow capsicums, quartered lengthwise and
  deseeded
3 large red capsicums, quartered lengthwise and
  deseeded
1 long eggplant, thinly sliced lengthwise
2 long zucchini, thinly sliced lengthwise

Preheat oven to 225F (110C). Mix garlic
with 2 tablespoons of the oil, and mix pesto
with remaining oil; set aside. Arrange
tomatoes on a baking sheet in a single layer
and sprinkle with salt. Bake for 4 hours.
Cool. Meanwhile, preheat broiler. Broil
capsicums until skins char and blister.
When cool enough to handle, peel off skins.
Brush pesto oil over eggplant slices and
garlic oil over zucchini slices. Broil in
batches in single layers until tender and
lightly browned.

Line a 4½ cup (35fl oz/1 litre) terrine with
plastic wrap leaving excess to cover top.
Layer vegetables alternately in terrine,
adding salt and pepper between each layer.
Fold excess plastic wrap over vegetables. Put
weights on top and chill for about 8 hours.
To serve, remove weights and top covering.
Invert terrine on to a board. Using a large,
sharp knife, cut into slices, then halve slices.
Pierce pieces with small skewers and arrange
on a serving dish.

Makes about 52

——BAKED POTATO WEDGES——

5 potatoes, unpeeled, each cut into 6 wedges
4 tablespoons lemon juice
4 tablespoons tomato paste
1 tablespoon ground coriander
2 teaspoons ground cumin
½ teaspoon ground chilies
salt
4 tablespoons groundnut oil
MANGO CHUTNEY DIP
⅔ cup (5fl oz/150ml) Greek-style yogurt
⅔ cup (5fl oz/150ml) mayonnaise
4-5 tablespoons mango chutney
3 tablespoons chopped fresh cilantro

Preheat oven to 350F (180C). To make dip, mix yogurt, mayonnaise, chutney, and chopped cilantro together. Cover until required. Put potatoes in a large bowl. In a smaller bowl, mix together remaining ingredients, except oil. Stir in 4 tablespoons water. Spoon tomato mixture over potatoes and stir to coat thoroughly and evenly.

Add oil to a roasting pan. Put potatoes and any remaining tomato mixture in pan. Stir to coat in oil. Bake for about 25 minutes, or until tender and a rich brown, shaking pan occasionally. Serve hot accompanied by mango chutney dip.

Makes 30

— CREAMY FENNEL-FILLED PUFFS —

¼ cup (2oz/50g) butter
generous ½ cup (2½oz/70g) all-purpose flour
2 eggs, lightly beaten
¾ cup (3oz/85g) grated Gruyère cheese
salt and freshly ground black pepper
1-2 tablespoons freshly grated Parmesan cheese
1 small fennel bulb, finely chopped
scant 1 cup (7oz/200g) medium fat cream cheese
lemon juice, to taste

Preheat oven to 400F (200C). Melt butter with ⅔ cup (5fl oz/150ml) water in a medium saucepan, then bring quickly to a boil. Immediately remove from heat and beat in flour all at once using a wooden spoon. Return pan to heat and beat for 1 minute, or until mixture comes away from sides of pan. Off the heat, gradually beat in eggs, beating well after each addition, until dough is shiny and drops easily from a lifted spoon. Beat in Gruyère cheese, and salt and pepper. Spoon into a pastry bag fitted with a plain tube.

Pipe 20 small blobs on to greased and dampened baking sheets, spacing them well apart. Sprinkle with Parmesan. Bake for 20-30 minutes until risen and golden. Remove from oven and make a small hole in side of each puff. Return to oven to dry out. Stir fennel into cream cheese, with lemon juice and salt and pepper to taste. Cut a diagonal slit in each puff, from top towards base. Fill with fennel mixture. Serve within 30 minutes.

Makes 20

FAVA BEAN FALAFEL

1lb (450g) frozen fava beans
2 teaspoons coriander seeds
2 teaspoons cumin seeds
2 teaspoons sesame seeds
leaves from 1 large bunch cilantro
leaves from 1 bunch flat-leaf parsley
1 red onion, chopped
2 cloves garlic, crushed
3 eggs
salt and freshly ground black pepper
flour for dusting
vegetable oil for deep-frying
DIP
¾ cup (6fl oz/175ml) Greek-style yogurt
3 tablespoons chopped fresh cilantro

Boil beans until tender. Drain well and put in a blender. Heat a small, dry pan, add seeds and fry for 2-3 minutes until fragrant. Add to beans, with herbs, red onion, and garlic. Purée bean mixture, adding eggs one at a time, to make a smooth paste. Season with salt and pepper. Chill for 45 minutes.

To make dip, stir together yogurt, cilantro, and salt and pepper. Cover and chill. With floured hands, shape tablespoons of bean mixture into balls, then flatten them slightly. Heat oil in a deep pan to 350F (180C). Deep-fry balls until crisp and brown, turning once. Drain on paper towels and keep warm. Serve with dip.

Makes about 16

—— MUSHROOMS EN CROÛTE ——

½ cup (4oz/115g) garlic and herb soft cheese
20 even-sized mushrooms, stalks removed
8 sheets of phyllo pastry
⅓ cup (3oz/85g) butter, melted
salt and freshly ground black pepper
1 egg, beaten

Preheat oven to 400F (200C). Divide cheese among cavities in mushrooms.

Brush 4 phyllo sheets with melted butter. Cover with remaining sheets. Brush with melted butter again. Cut phyllo sheets into 20 squares.

Put a mushroom, cheese side up, in center of each square. Season with salt and pepper. Lift sides of pastry over mushrooms to resemble small sacks and pinch neck edges together to seal. Place on a greased baking sheet and brush with beaten egg. Bake for about 15 minutes until pastry is crisp and golden. Serve hot.

Makes 20

── BAKED NEW POTATOES ──

3¼-3½lb (1.5kg) small new potatoes, unpeeled
4 tablespoons soy sauce
2 tablespoons peanut oil
2 tablespoons sesame oil
4 tablespoons lemon juice
1oz (25g) sesame seeds
1 cup (8oz/225g) mayonnaise
grated rind and juice of 1 lime
2 teaspoons grated fresh root ginger
2 tablespoons chopped fresh cilantro
finely chopped green part of scallions, to garnish

Preheat oven to 400F (200C). In a saucepan of boiling, salted water, cook potatoes for 5 minutes. Drain well. Put in a roasting pan. Trickle soy sauce, oils, and lemon juice over and stir together. Sprinkle with sesame seeds. Bake for about 45 minutes or until tender.

In a bowl, mix together mayonnaise, lime rind and juice, ginger, and cilantro. Halve the potatoes lengthwise. With a melon baller or teaspoon, scoop out a hollow in each potato half. Fill with mayonnaise mixture. Serve garnished with finely chopped scallions.

Makes about 28

EGGPLANT BASKETS

2 large eggplants
3 cloves garlic, crushed
1½ tablespoons lime juice
2 teaspoons ground cumin
3 tablespoon chopped fresh cilantro
3 tablespoons olive oil
8 sun-dried tomatoes, drained and chopped
16 pitted black olives, finely chopped
freshly ground black pepper
1 package mini pappadoms, about 40
cilantro sprigs, and paprika (optional), to garnish

Preheat oven to 400F (200C). Cut several slits in eggplants then bake for about 1 hour or until very soft. Allow to cool. Cut eggplants open, scoop out flesh and wrap in a clean cloth. Squeeze hard to remove moisture.

Put eggplant flesh in a bowl and mash well with garlic, lime juice, cumin, and cilantro. Stir in olive oil, sun-dried tomatoes and olives. Season with black pepper. Cover and leave until required. Spoon into the pappadoms and garnish with cilantro sprigs, and paprika, if using.

Makes 40

ZUCCHINI DROPS

3 small zucchini, total weight 12oz (350g), grated
olive oil for frying
1 small onion, grated
1 clove garlic, finely crushed (optional)
small bunch of fresh parsley, finely chopped
salt and freshly ground black pepper
3 eggs, beaten
TOPPING
1 avocado, pitted
½ cup (4oz/115g) cream cheese
2 scallions, very finely chopped
grated rind and juice of 1 lime
1½ tablespoons chopped fresh mint
mint leaves, or finely diced red capsicum, to garnish

To make topping, mash ingredients together. Season to taste with salt and pepper. Cover and chill for 1-2 hours. Add zucchini to a large pan of boiling water, return to the boil then drain well. Dry thoroughly on paper towels. Heat a little oil in a skillet, and fry onion until soft and golden. Add garlic, if using, and fry for 2-3 minutes. Drain on paper towels. Mix zucchini, onion mixture, parsley, and salt and pepper with eggs.

Heat a little oil in a large, heavy skillet. Drop large teaspoonfuls of mixture into oil and fry for 2-3 minutes until golden underneath. Turn over and brown for about 2 minutes. Transfer to paper towels to drain. Repeat with the remaining mixture. Put small spoonfuls of topping on each zucchini drop, to serve. Garnish with mint leaves or finely diced red capsicum.

Makes about 40

— VIETNAMESE CORN FRITTERS —

1¼ cups (5oz/150g) all-purpose flour
1 teaspoon baking powder
2 eggs, beaten
2 tablespoons soy sauce
2 tablespoons lime juice
grated rind of 2 limes
2 tablespoons chopped fresh cilantro
1¾ cup (10oz/300g) frozen corn kernels, thawed
vegetable oil for deep frying
about 32 Belgian endive leaves, to serve
cilantro leaves, to garnish
SAUCE
4 tablespoons white wine vinegar
4 tablespoons superfine sugar
1 teaspoon dried chili flakes
salt and freshly ground black pepper

In a bowl, beat together flour, baking powder, eggs, soy sauce, and lime juice and rind. Stir in cilantro and corn. Set aside. To make sauce, in a small saucepan, gently heat vinegar, sugar, chili flakes, salt and pepper, and 2 tablespoons water until sugar dissolves. Bring to a boil, then remove from heat and let cool.

In a deep, wide saucepan, heat 2in (5cm) depth of oil until a cube of bread crisps in 30 seconds. Add spoonfuls of corn mixture in batches and fry for 2-3 minutes. Drain on paper towels. Put a warm fritter in each Belgian endive leaf and spear with a toothpick. Trickle a little sauce over and garnish with cilantro leaves.

Makes about 32

VEGETABLE CRISPS

3¼-3½lb (1.5kg) mixed vegetables such as parsnips,
  celery root, sweet potato, kohlrabi, raw beets,
  peeled
vegetable oil for deep frying
sea salt
paprika, freshly grated Parmesan cheese, or ground
  chilies for sprinkling

Using a potato peeler, slice vegetables very
thinly, keeping different types separate.
Keep completely covered in cold water until
required. Drain and dry thoroughly with
paper towels.

Heat some oil in a deep-fryer to 350F
(180C). Fry vegetable ribbons in small
batches until crisp and golden, turning
occasionally. Drain on paper towels.

Sprinkle with salt and flavorings of your
choice. Repeat with remaining vegetables.
Pile into baskets or bowls to serve.

Makes about 2lb (1kg)

MUSHROOM ROLLS

5 tablespoons sesame oil
4 shallots, finely chopped
1 plump clove garlic, crushed
4 teaspoons grated fresh root ginger
1lb (450g) shiitake mushrooms, coarsely chopped
2 teaspoons five-spice powder
salt and freshly ground black pepper
24 sheets phyllo pastry
sunflower oil for brushing

In a skillet, heat oil. Add shallots and garlic and fry for 2-3 minutes. Stir in ginger and mushrooms and cook for about 5 minutes, until tender. Add five-spice powder, and salt and pepper. Allow to cool.

Preheat oven to 425F (220C). Brush 1 phyllo sheet with sunflower oil. Spoon a little of the mushroom mixture near a short edge and roll up, folding in the edges. Place on a baking sheet. Repeat with remaining pastry and filling. Brush with oil and bake for 15 minutes or until crisp. Serve warm.

Makes 24

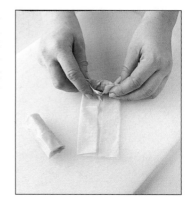

MUSHROOM BRIOCHE

3 tablespoons (1½oz/40g) butter
1 clove garlic, crushed
10oz (300g) brown cap mushrooms, or small wild
    mushrooms, coarsely chopped
1 teaspoon Dijon mustard
2 teaspoons thyme leaves
salt and freshly ground black pepper
20 mini brioches

In a large skillet, heat butter. Add garlic and
mushrooms and cook, stirring occasionally,
for 4-5 minutes, or until tender. Stir in
mustard, thyme, and salt and pepper. Let
cool.

Preheat oven to 350F (180C). Cut tops off
brioches, reserving lids. Using a melon
baller or teaspoon, scoop out insides of each
brioche, taking care not to pierce sides and
base. (Use insides for bread crumbs.)

Place brioches on a baking sheet. Spoon in
mushroom mixture and replace lids. Cover
loosely with foil and put in oven for 6-7
minutes. Serve warm.

Makes 20

SAVORY SQUARES

3 cups (12oz/350g) bread flour
1½ teaspoons fast rising yeast
2 tablespoons chopped mixed fresh herbs
salt and freshly ground black pepper
1 tablespoon olive oil
2 tablespoons red pesto
2oz (50g) thinly sliced prosciutto
5oz (150g) mozzarella cheese, grated
2 tablespoons pitted black olives, chopped
1 egg yolk, beaten with 1 tablespoon water
coarse sea salt for sprinkling

In a large bowl, stir together flour, yeast, herbs, and salt and pepper. Add oil and scant 1 cup (7fl oz/200ml) water and mix to a soft dough. Turn on to a lightly floured surface and knead for about 10 minutes, or until smooth and elastic. Roll out half the dough to line a greased 9x13in (23x33cm) jelly roll pan. Spread with red pesto and cover with prosciutto slices.

Scatter mozzarella and then olives over. Brush edges of dough lightly with beaten egg. Roll out remaining dough to cover filling. Press edges lightly together. Brush top with beaten egg and sprinkle coarse salt over. Leave for about 30 minutes, or until puffy. Preheat oven to 425F (220C). Bake for 20-25 minutes until browned and crisp. Leave to cool in pan for 5 minutes, then cut into 5 strips lengthwise and 10 strips crosswise. Serve warm.

Makes 50

RÖSTI

¼ cup (2oz/50g) butter
8oz (225g) onion, finely chopped
1lb (450g) potatoes, grated, soaked in cold water
4 eggs, beaten
3 tablespoons chopped fresh parsley or cilantro
salt and freshly ground black pepper
olive oil for frying
¾ cup (6oz/175g) soft goats' cheese
3 tablespoons sour cream
parsley or cilantro sprigs, to garnish

Heat the butter in a skillet. Add onion and fry for about 5 minutes, or until soft. Drain potatoes and dry thoroughly. Put into a bowl. Mix with eggs, onion, parsley or cilantro, and salt and pepper. In a large, heavy-based skillet, heat oil.

Fry teaspoonfuls of potato mixture in batches for 2-3 minutes on each side or until golden and crisp. Drain on paper towels. Keep in a cool place until required. Beat together goats' cheese, sour cream, and salt and pepper. Cover and chill. To serve, preheat oven to 400F (200C). Put rösti on baking sheets, cover loosely with foil and warm through for about 4 minutes. Top with cheese mixture. Garnish with herb sprigs and serve.

Makes about 60

GRISSINI

4 cups (1lb/450g) bread flour
1 sachet fast rising yeast
2 tablespoons oil from jar of sun-dried tomatoes in
   oil, or virgin olive oil
1¼ cups (10fl oz/300ml) warm water
virgin olive oil for greasing
6 tablespoons chopped fresh basil
8 tablespoons roughly chopped black olives
DIP
3 large red capsicums, halved and deseeded
5 cloves garlic, unpeeled
scant 1 cup (7oz/200g) reduced-fat soft cheese
½ teaspoon hot pepper sauce
salt and freshly ground black pepper

To make dip, preheat broiler. Broil
capsicums until skins are charred and
blistered, and garlic until soft and charred.
When cool enough to handle, peel off skins.
Purée capsicums and garlic with cheese, and
salt and pepper in a blender. Cover and
refrigerate for at least 2 hours. Stir flour, salt
and pepper, and yeast together. Stir in oil
and water and beat to a soft but not sticky
dough. Knead for about 10 minutes until
smooth and elastic. Put into an oiled bowl.
Turn to coat with oil, cover and leave until
doubled in volume.

Preheat oven to 400F (200C). Halve dough.
On a lightly floured surface, knead basil into
one half, and olives into other half. Divide
each piece into 16. Roll out pieces in turn
to pencil shapes about 9in (23cm) long.
Transfer to baking sheets. Bake for 15-20
minutes, or until golden and crisp. Remove
to a wire rack to cool. Serve with the dip.

Makes 32

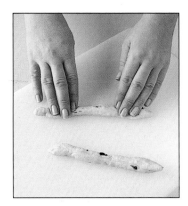

MINI PIZZAS

4 cups (1lb/450g) bread flour, plus extra for dusting
1 sachet fast rising yeast
salt and freshly ground black pepper
scant 1 cup (7fl oz/200ml) warm water
2 tablespoons virgin olive oil, plus extra for brushing
virgin olive oil for greasing
TOPPING
2 tablespoons virgin olive oil
2 shallots, finely chopped
2 cloves garlic, finely crushed
1lb (450g) mixed brown, shiitake and oyster
  mushrooms, diced
1 tablespoon chopped fresh tarragon
9oz (250g) jar hollandaise sauce

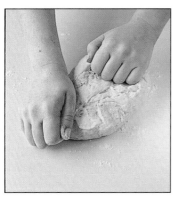

In a large mixing bowl, stir together flour, yeast, and salt and pepper. Gradually stir in warm water and oil and beat to a soft but not wet dough. Turn on to a lightly floured surface and knead for 10 minutes, until smooth and elastic.

Put into an oiled bowl, cover with plastic wrap and leave until doubled in volume.

To make topping, heat oil in a skillet, add shallots and cook until tender and lightly browned. Stir in garlic and mushrooms and cook for a further 5 minutes or until all the liquid has evaporated. Add tarragon, and salt and pepper to taste. Set aside.

Preheat oven to 450F (230C). Oil 2 baking sheets. Punch down dough and knead briefly. Divide into 16 pieces. Roll each piece to ¼in (5mm) thick circle.

Transfer dough circles to baking sheets. Brush with virgin olive oil. Spoon on mushroom mixture. Bake for about 10 minutes or until bases are crisp and browned. Preheat broiler. Spoon hollandaise sauce on to pizzas and put briefly under broiler until glazed.

Makes 16

MEXICAN MINI MUFFINS

¾ cup (6oz/175g) butter, softened
¾ cup (6oz/175g) cream cheese
2 small eggs
1 cup (4oz/115g) each self-rising flour and cornmeal
pinch of baking powder
salt and freshly ground black pepper
1 red capsicum, deseeded and finely chopped
GUACAMOLE
3 large avocados, pitted
1 clove garlic, finely crushed
1½ tablespoons finely chopped red onion
¼ teaspoon ground cumin
pinch of ground chilies
juice of 1 lime
3 tablespoons chopped fresh cilantro
1 large tomato, deseeded and finely chopped

Preheat oven to 350F (180C). Grease 40 mini muffin pans. Beat butter and cheese together then beat in eggs. Mix flour, cornmeal, baking powder, and salt and pepper together then gradually stir into butter mixture. Add red capsicum. Spoon into pans and bake for 20 minutes or until golden.

Meanwhile, make guacamole. Mash avocados with garlic, red onion, spices, and lime juice. Stir in cilantro and tomato. Season to taste with salt and pepper. Serve muffins warm, accompanied by a bowl of guacamole.

Makes about 40

ORANGE TRUFFLE CUPS

9oz (250g) dark chocolate, grated
1 egg yolk
1 tablespoon unsalted butter
1 tablespoon finely grated orange rind
scant ½ cup (3½fl oz/100ml) heavy cream, whipped
fine strips peel from marmalade, to decorate

Put half the chocolate into a heatproof bowl over a saucepan of hot water. Stir occasionally until chocolate has melted.

Using a small pastry brush or paint brush, brush melted chocolate over inside of paper petit-four cases. Leave to set then repeat and leave until firm. Make a small tear in paper case then carefully peel off.

Meanwhile, in a heatproof bowl over a pan of hot water, warm remaining chocolate until almost melted. Add egg yolk and stir until thickened. Remove bowl from heat and stir in butter and orange rind. Set aside to cool to room temperature. Fold in cream and spoon into a pastry bag fitted with a star tube. Pipe filling neatly into each chocolate case. Decorate with peel from marmalade.

Makes 24

LIME TARTLETS

1½ cups (6oz/175g) all-purpose flour
¾ cup (3oz/85g) ground almonds
2 tablespoons superfine sugar
½ cup (4oz/115g) butter, diced
1 egg yolk
FILLING
4 eggs
½ cup (4oz/115g) superfine sugar
2 tablespoons crème fraîche or sour cream
⅔ cup (5fl oz/150ml) lime juice
DECORATION
thinly pared rind of lime
2½ tablespoons superfine sugar

Stir flour, ground almonds, and sugar together in a bowl. Rub in butter until mixture resembles fine bread crumbs. Add egg yolk and 1-2 tablespoons cold water and mix to a dough. Knead briefly, cover and chill.

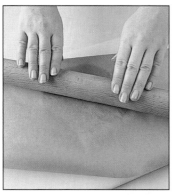

Put dough on a lightly floured surface. Cover with baking parchment. Roll in one direction to ¼in (5mm) thick.

Preheat oven to 375F (190C). Cut out rounds using a 2in (5cm) cutter; gently press into tartlet pans. Lightly prick shells. Chill for 30 minutes. Bake for 10 minutes. Cool. (Leave oven on.)

To make filling, whisk together eggs and sugar. Stir in crème fraîche or sour cream and lime juice until evenly combined. Pour into tartlet cases. Bake for 15 minutes, or until filling is set. Serve warm or cold.

To make decoration, cut lemon rind into short, fine strips. Blanch for 2 minutes in boiling water. Drain. In a small pan, gently heat sugar in 2 tablespoons water until dissolved. Add lime strips and simmer for 8-10 minutes until strips are transparent and water has evaporated. Remove strips with a slotted spoon. Decorate tops of tarts before serving.

Makes 24

—— NUT & COFFEE MERINGUES ——

2 egg whites
½ cup (4oz/115g) superfine sugar
½ cup (2oz/50g) ground walnuts
chocolate-coated coffee beans, and pecan halves,
   to decorate
FILLING
scant 1 cup (7fl oz/about 200ml) heavy cream
about 1 tablespoon confectioners' sugar, sifted
about 1 teaspoon espresso coffee powder

Preheat oven to 250F (120C). Cover baking sheets with baking parchment. Whisk egg whites until stiff. Gradually add sugar, whisking constantly, and continue to whisk until mixture is very stiff and shiny. Gently fold in ground walnuts. Spoon into a pastry bag fitted with a plain tube and pipe about 45 small discs of meringue on the baking sheets. Bake for about 1 hour until dry, very lightly colored and can be lifted easily from baking parchment. Cool on a wire rack.

To make filling, whip cream with sugar and coffee to taste. Just before serving, pipe a small swirl of cream on each base. Decorate some with chocolate-coated coffee beans and some with pecan halves. Serve in small paper cases.

Makes about 45

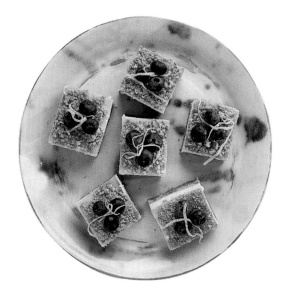

CHEESECAKE SQUARES

⅓ cup (3oz/85g) butter, diced
1¼ cups (5oz/150g) self-rising flour
2oz (50g) amaretti biscuits, finely crushed
¼ cup (2oz/50g) plus 1 tablespoon superfine sugar
1 egg yolk plus 2 eggs, separated
1 cup (8oz/225g) mascarpone cheese
1 cup (8oz/225g) ricotta cheese
1 tablespoon cornstarch
grated rind of 1 lemon
1 tablespoon rum
2oz (50g) amaretti biscuits, in coarse crumbs
raspberries, blueberries, or sliced strawberries, to
  decorate

Preheat oven to 400F (200C). Grease and
base-line a shallow 8in (20cm) square cake
pan. Rub butter into flour until mixture
resembles fine bread crumbs. Stir in finely
crushed amaretti and 1 tablespoon superfine
sugar. Mix to a dough with 1 egg yolk, plus a
little water if necessary. Knead lightly. With
finger-tips, press dough into base of pan.
Cover with foil and top with raw rice or
baking beans. Bake for 10 minutes.

To make filling, beat cheeses together then
mix in remaining superfine sugar, egg yolks,
cornstarch, lemon rind, and rum. Whisk egg
whites until stiff then carefully fold into
cheese mixture. Pour on to pastry base.
Sprinkle amaretti crumbs over top and bake
just below center of oven for 1¼ hours until
just firm in center. Leave to cool in oven
with heat turned off. Cut into small squares.
Decorate each square with a raspberry,
blueberry or a strawberry slice.

Makes about 64

——— SPICED HOT FRUIT KABOBS ———

2¼lb (1kg) prepared mixed fresh fruits such as
  mango, papaya, pineapple, nectarine, plum, banana,
  lychees, cherries
⅔ cup (5oz/150g) unsalted butter
3 tablespoons grated fresh root ginger
1 tablespoon confectioners' sugar
1 tablespoon lime juice

Soak about 20 bamboo skewers in water for
30 minutes. Cut fruit into bite-size chunks.
Thread a selection of fruits on each skewer.

Melt butter and stir in ginger, confectioners'
sugar, and lime juice.

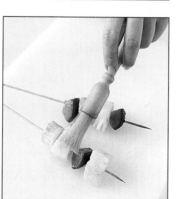

Brush over kabobs. Preheat broiler. Cook
kabobs, turning frequently and brushing
with butter mixture, for about 5 minutes
until beginning to caramelize. Serve warm.

Makes about 20

— CHOCOLATE MINI MUFFINS —

1¼ cups (5oz/150g) self-rising flour
2½ tablespoons cocoa powder
1 teaspoon baking powder
pinch of salt
¼ cup (2oz/50g) light brown sugar
1 small egg, lightly beaten
⅔ cup (5fl oz/150ml) milk
¼ cup (2oz/50g) butter, melted and cooled slightly
½ teaspoon vanilla extract
chocolate and hazelnut spread or chocolate frosting,
    for filling

Preheat oven to 400F (200C). Grease 20 mini muffin cups, about 1¾x¼in (4.5x0.5cm), or put small paper cases in cups.

Sift flour, cocoa powder, baking powder, and salt into a shallow bowl. Stir in sugar. Stir egg into milk, butter, and vanilla extract. Pour on to dry ingredients and mix briefly using a large metal spoon and a lifting figure-of-eight movement; there should not be any free flour but mixture should still be lumpy.

One third- to half-fill paper cases or muffin tins with mixture. Put ½-1 teaspoon of spread or frosting on each portion of mixture and cover with more mixture so that cases or cups are almost filled. Bake for 20 minutes until risen and tops spring back when lightly touched. Paper cases can be removed immediately; alternatively, place cups on a wire rack and leave to cool for 5 minutes, then remove muffins from cups. Serve warm.

Makes about 20

INDEX